What they don't tell you about

ELIZA

HER FRIENDS

AND RELATIONS

By Bob Fowke

Dedicated to clever girls with
long pointed noses everywhere.

*Hodder
Children's
Books*

a division of Hodder Headline plc

Hallo, my name's Harry Hunks. I'm a bear, a famous fighting bear. It's *grrrrrrrrreat* to meet you. I know a lot about the reign of Elizabeth I from all the different kinds of people who came to watch me fight in the bear ring. Elizabeth was no *honey*, but she and her friends were furociously fascinating. So come with me and find out more about her. We may only *scratch* the surface of her story, but there's plenty of amazing facts to *bite* into if you read on...

Produced by Lazy Summer Books for Hodder Children's Books

Text and illustrations by Bob Fowke

Cover portrait of Elizabeth I by M. Gheeraerts the Younger courtesy of the National Portrait Gallery, London.

Published by Hodder Children's Books 1995

10 9 8 7 6 5 4 3 2 1

ISBN 0340 65613 1

Hodder Children's Books
a Division of Hodder Headline plc
338 Euston Road
London NW1 3BH

Printed and bound by Cox & Wyman Ltd, Reading, Berks
A Catalogue record for this book is available from the British Library

CONTENTS

LOOK OUT FOR THE LANKY LADY! Page 5
How it all began

KIDS STUFF Page 11
But you won't like it

TEEN SCENES Page 19
Sister squabbles – need we say more

HOME COMFORTS Page 25
Palaces that pong and other wonders

LEISURE PLEASURES Page 32
Having fun, the tudor way

DASHING DUDLEY, DEMON LOVER Page 43
Fancy clothes and free women

OFF WITH HER HEAD! Page 52
Scottish mary and the multiple murders

WORKERS AND SHIRKERS Page 61
Gizza job, Liz!

 Whenever you see this sign in the book it means there are some more details at the FOOT of the page, like here.

LONDON LOUTS AND HARD BARDS
Page 72

WILL SHAKESPEARE AND THE ACTOR FACTOR

LOADS OF LOOT
Page 83

POSH PIRATES ON THE SEVEN SEAS

ARMADA!
Page 97

TRY HARDER ARMADA

TROUBLESOME TOYBOY
Page 105

HE CLIMBED TOO HIGH

GOOODBYE ELIZABETH
Page 112

THE FINAL CHAPTER – ALMOST

WHAT HAPPENED NEXT
Page 118

WELL, A BIT OF IT

STATE THE DATE
Page 119

GLORIANA AT A GLANCE

GRAND QUIZ
Page 121

TEST YOUR TUDOR EXPERTISE

INDEX
Page 125

NOW READ ON
Page 128

MORE BOOKS ON GOOD QUEEN BESS

WATCH OUT FOR THE LANKY LADY!

How It All Began

It's two o'clock in the morning one day in 1601, bedtime for most honest citizens. A bony old woman prowls around her private room. Every now and then she pauses, muttering, and stabs a rusty sword deep into the rich wall-hangings. She fears that enemies lurk in the shadows behind, waiting to kill her.

BRIGHT ORANGE WIG

BAD SKIN DUE TO USING TOO MUCH MERCURY AND TURPENTINE MAKE-UP.

BAD TEETH DUE TO THE NEW FASHION OF EATING A LOT OF SUGAR.

The old lady is Elizabeth I, the last of the Tudors and the greatest Queen of England ever.

How did it all begin?...

Buttered baby

It all started one Sunday in September 1533, at Greenwich Palace on the south bank of the river Thames, where Queen Anne Boleyn lay in her royal bed. The midwives, who help at births, had trimmed their nails and smeared pig-fat or butter on their hands to make them slippery, ready to help deliver a new royal baby.

But wait –
Two reasons to be nervous:

1. The father-to-be was King Henry VIII and he wanted a boy to inherit his crown.

2. Henry VIII had a very bad temper.

The new baby arrived at around four in the afternoon. As soon as people heard the news, church bells were pealed and bonfires were lit in celebration of the birth. The crowd went wild, but in all the happy throng two people weren't celebrating; Henry and Anne were fed up – the baby was a little girl.

FAMILY GALLERY

Baby Elizabeth was Henry's second royal child. His eldest was Mary, daughter of Henry's first wife.

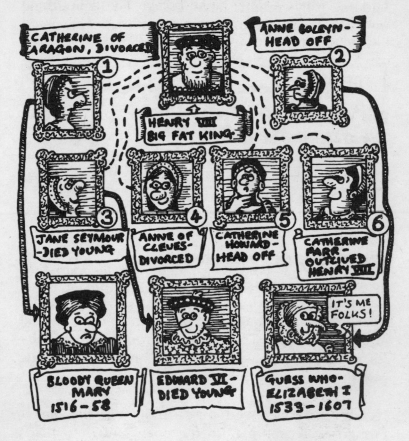

CATHERINE OF ARAGON, DIVORCED ①

HENRY VIII BIG FAT KING

ANNE BOLEYN - HEAD OFF ②

JANE SEYMOUR - DIED YOUNG ③

ANNE OF CLEVES - DIVORCED ④

CATHERINE HOWARD - HEAD OFF ⑤

CATHERINE PARR - OUTLIVED HENRY VIII ⑥

BLOODY QUEEN MARY 1516-58

EDWARD VI - DIED YOUNG

GUESS WHO - ELIZABETH I 1533-1607

IT'S ME FOLKS!

Henry had one other child called Henry Fitzroy by a mistress called Bessie Blount. He died when he was seventeen, poor cub.

7

NAME GAMES

Elizabeth was christened when she was three days old. Her parents nearly called her Mary although, being Tudors, they might have called her something unusual. Tudor people liked fancy names, such as these:

Temperance Slaughter
Appelina Proudlove
Cognata Stocker
Cassandra Potter

VAGAMONKS AND VAGABONDS

Soon after the baptism, because her mother was busy being Queen of England, Elizabeth was sent away to the country to be looked after by an aunt. The country through which baby Elizabeth was carried to her aunt's house was in the middle of some big changes.

Nearly everyone lived by farming, but the bigger farmers were carving up the open land into fields surrounded by hedges or walls. The area of common land left over for poor men to farm was shrinking. Hordes of landless men were forced to wander the countryside as vagabonds. On top of that, Henry had recently decided to shut all the monasteries and take their riches. So unemployed monks joined the hordes of vagabonds.

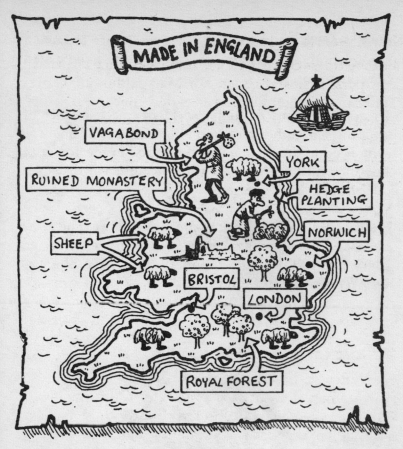

A CHOP OFF THE OLD BLOCK

QUESTION:
What do you do if your name is Henry VIII and your wife doesn't give birth to a son?

ANSWER:
Chop her head off.

When Elizabeth was one-year-old, her mother Anne nearly had a baby boy, but this little nearly-brother died before he was born. From then on Henry gave up on Anne. He looked round for a new wife to have a son for him, and he soon found a girl he liked called Jane Seymour.

To get Anne out of the way, Henry accused her of sleeping with other men and after a short trial she was sentenced to death. She was beheaded at the Tower of London on 19th May 1536. They brought a swordsman over from France specially.

Henry divorced Anne two days before she was beheaded. So now Elizabeth as well as her elder sister, Mary, had lost her right to inherit the throne. She was two years and eight months old.

KID'S STUFF

– BUT YOU WON'T LIKE IT

Elizabeth had plenty of time for her education. It was quite common for young royals to learn more than one language, but Elizabeth was extra brainy. She learned to speak lots of them.

GREEK- QUITE WELL

FRENCH- FLUENTLY

WELSH - NOT MUCH

ENGLISH (OF COURSE)

ITALIAN- FLUENTLY

SPANISH- A LITTLE

FLEMISH- NOT MUCH

LATIN- FLUENTLY

GIRLS' SKOOL

During Elizabeth's childhood most middle and upper class girls learned to read and write. This was because

there were lots of books around due to the invention of printing. Books on subjects like cookery, household management and needlework started to be written specially for women.

Girls' education could be tough. Many teachers believed that it was important to beat girls as well as boys – especially girls, according to the tutor of Elizabeth's older sister, Mary. (Elizabeth was luckier; her tutor didn't believe in that sort of thing).

Most working-class girls never got the chance to learn to read and write at all, but even rich girls didn't have to learn quite as much as Elizabeth. I picked up this timetable which some young aristocrat dropped into the bear-pit...

As well as languages and subjects like dancing and music, Elizabeth had to learn maths, history, geography, architecture and astronomy. She ended up knowing a lot more than most upper-class boys.

BOYS' SKOOL
TWO QUESTIONS...

1. Do you hate school?

2. Are you a boy?

If the answer to both questions is yes – count your blessings, brother. You would have hated school a lot more if you had been a Tudor. Girls were taught at home, but boys' schools were really tough. School started as early as five or six in the morning and went on till five or six at night, with two hours for lunch.

THE TUDOR CLASS-ROOM

Flogging and other physical punishments were a normal part of school life. These are some typical Tudor punishments:

1. being pulled by the hair ▸

14

2. being lashed over the face ◄

3. being beaten about the head with a great rod ◢

4. being struck on the lips with a ruler. ►

Animals were punished too. People thought that, just like children, it was good for their characters. For instance a dog which killed a lamb might be locked up with a fierce ram to teach it better manners.

DON'T SPEAK TILL YOU'RE SPOKEN TO!

Being a royal, Elizabeth had her own household, even though she was young. She was treated with respect by the people who looked after her. She was lucky; in all non-royal houses young people had to be very careful how they behaved.

Amaze your parents. Try out this Tudor guide to good behaviour...

TUDOR KIDS

Stand up in the presence of your parents.

Call your parents Sir and Madame.

Eat at a separate table.

Serve your parents at table, if there are no servants to do it.

YOUR SERVANT, SIR

A lot of servants were needed to run big houses. Most of them were young people who were not always much older than the children of the house. The master and mistress were responsible for their young servants, as they were for their own children. Nearly three quarters of all boys and more than half of all girls between the ages of twenty and twenty-four were servants. There were more boys than girls because boys were useful for defence, as armed retainers. Most country villages only had a handful of young men living in them. The rest were away working as servants in towns or big houses.

Even the rich sent their children to serve in other people's houses as pages or sometimes as ladies in waiting. Servants and their masters lived closely together. In fact stewards and other top servants were more like courtiers or friends. Elizabeth always had a number of people like this living with her. Her ladies-in-waiting were always noble women.

SERVANT RULES

There were still rules to be followed. For example:

1. People 'gave the wall' to their superiors if they met them in the street. This meant letting them have the side of the pavement furthest away from passing horses and carts.

2. Servants called their master and mistress by their full name and title ➤.

3. Masters and Mistresses called their servants by their first names.

4. Servants could be fined if they did wrong:

One penny	swearing, untidy dress, leaving a bed unmade after 8.00am
Two pennies	not going to family prayers
Six pennies	being late to serve dinner

 The terms 'Mr' and 'Mrs' are shortened forms of Master and Mistress.

If you couldn't play with other children, there were always animals to play with. Tudor houses were full of them and Tudor kids had time to play even though their hours of work were long.

CAT FANATICS AND DOG SNOBS

Hounds and spaniels were the top dogs. There were clear class distinctions. For instance, in 1567 the Mayor of Liverpool ordered that all mastiffs (a large fierce dog) and watchdogs had to be tied up so that they didn't hurt any posh hounds.

Tabbies were the top cats because only the rich could afford them. The first tabbies had only recently been brought to England from the East. Whatever their class, pets were often very well treated. One merchant in Leeds had holes cut through all the doors in his house so that his cats could wander freely.

WARNING TO TUDOR CATS

Not everyone liked cats. One school book had this simple sentence in Latin for translation: 'I hate cats'.

TEEN SCENES

WOULD YOU LIKE TO BE YOUR FATHER'S WIDOW'S WIDOWER'S WIFE?

Henry VIII died in 1547. He was succeeded by his son, Edward, Elizabeth's younger brother. Being a girl, Elizabeth never expected to become Queen.

While all this was happening Elizabeth was looked after by Henry's widow, Catherine Parr, who remarried, this time to handsome, red-bearded Lord Thomas Seymour. Teenage Elizabeth had a crush on teasing Lord Thomas. He used to make her laugh; once he and Catherine chased her round the garden then cut her gown into little pieces.

Catherine died in childbirth in 1548, and soon afterwards Thomas asked Elizabeth to marry him. As Elizabeth's husband he would have a chance of becoming King if young King Edward died. She put him off saying she was not ready. Desperate for power, Thomas then plotted to kidnap Edward.

Thomas' plots were discovered. He was beheaded on 20th March 1549.

Spot The Difference!

Catholic Mary

Young King Edward VI didn't last long. He died on 6th July 1553 of a disease called tuberculosis. Within days Elizabeth's elder sister, Mary, was made Queen. Mary was a staunch Roman Catholic.

PROTESTANT ELIZABETH

Elizabeth was a Protestant. Once Mary came to the throne, Elizabeth was in danger. Mary was determined to stamp out all traces of Protestantism in England and started on a programme of burning Protestants.

SQUASH THE PROTS!

In 1553, when Edward died and Mary came to the throne, Europe was about to be torn apart in a deadly war between Catholics and Protestants.

Catholics hated Protestants because Protestants had turned their backs on the Roman Catholic church. They burned and tortured them to try to turn them into Catholics. Protestants hated Catholics because they thought that the Roman Catholic religion was corrupt. Protestants burned and tortured too, although not so much.

To make matters worse there was a new hard-line breed of Protestant. These were the Puritans. They wore dark clothes, went to church a lot and disapproved of people having fun. Elizabeth was never a Puritan even though she was a Protestant.

A party of prim Puritans

Some visitors to my show dropped these newspaper cuttings. I picked them up so you could have a look...

The Elizabethan Echo

DUTCH IN FREEDOM FIGHT– 1568

The Netherlands was part of the Spanish Empire. Most Dutch people were Protestants and their Spanish rulers tried to burn them back into the Catholic Church. In 1568 the Dutch started the revolt which would lead to Holland becoming an independent country.

HUGUENOTS HAMMERED 1562-98

French Protestants were called Huguenots. There were lots of them in France. They were unpopular, and the French government tried to crush them. The Wars of Religion went on for thirty-six years and forced many of the best French Protestants to leave the country.

PROT QUEEN CROWNED 1558

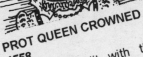

Henry VIII split with the Pope, but he was never a true Protestant. Edward had been a Protestant king, but too young to rule. It was only after Elizabeth came to power that England became the most powerful of all the Protestant countries.

PARIS PROTS MASSACRED – 1572

On 24th August, Saint Bartholomew's Day, 3000 Huguenots were massacred in cold blood in Paris, and many more in the French provinces. This event sent shock-waves through England.

Queen Mary's health was bad and if Mary died, Elizabeth would become the next Queen of England. Elizabeth was accused of plotting against her sister and sent to the Tower of London. For two months she was shut up and in daily fear of being beheaded. Her prison cell was a gloomy room opposite a passageway leading to three toilets which hung high over the walls of the moat.

Desperately Elizabeth pleaded for her life, and at last she was allowed to leave the Tower. It had been a narrow escape.

While Mary's health got worse, Elizabeth was shut up in a house in the country At last, one morning in 1558, a messenger galloped from London to where she was staying. He carried Mary's engagement ring – proof that Mary had died of cancer.

GREAT, SHE'S SNUFFED IT!

Very important nobles whose presence was inconvenient were quite often kept under 'house arrest' like this, rather than being imprisoned like a criminal.

HOME COMFORTS

A MAGIC MOMENT

Elizabeth believed in astrology . She asked the famous scientist Dr John Dee to tell her the best day for her coronation. Although Dr Dee was a scientist, he liked to dabble in magic and astrology as well. He had a crazy friend called Kelly who wore a black cap to hide the fact that his ears had been cut off . Egged on by Kelly, Dr Dee would try to read messages from spirits in a crystal ball. He chose Sunday 15th January for the coronation.

So on Sunday 15th January 1559 the crown of England was placed on Elizabeth's head in Westminster Abbey. Outside the crowd went wild; people were delighted to have a Protestant queen after bloody, Catholic Queen Mary. Bells peeled and brightly coloured hangings fluttered from every

---

 Astrologists believe that the position of the stars in the sky affects how things happen on Earth.

 Cutting off bits of the body was a common punishment for theft.

window in London. People fought to cut out bits from a posh blue carpet which had been laid for Elizabeth to walk over from Westminster Hall to Westminster Abbey. The Duchess of Norfolk, who was holding up Elizabeth's cloak, kept tripping over the holes in the carpet.

PALACES THAT PONG

Now that she was Queen, Elizabeth took possession of at least six palaces:

Richmond; good for hunting

Whitehall with its grounds, the largest palace in Europe

Greenwich by the river Thames

Hampton Court, stolen by old king Henry

Nonsuch built by old king Henry

There were about 1,500 people in the royal household, so the palaces got very crowded. The floors of the great halls were covered in rushes, and the rushes became disgustingly sticky with bits of food and dog mess. Things soon got very smelly. After about six weeks it was time to move on. Then all the mess could be shovelled out and the palace generally cleaned and 'sweetened'.

The royal court travelled from one palace to another with side-journeys to visit the houses of rich nobles further away. When on the move, the court travelled about twelve miles a day. All the furniture came too;

If Elizabeth came to visit and your house wasn't big enough, some of the courtiers and servants camped in the grounds or lodged in nearby villages and towns. It could cost you a pot of money.

four hundred wagons and 2,400 pack horses were needed to carry everything.

A ROOM AT THE TOP

In Elizabeth's time things were getting more comfortable than they had been in the past, especially at court and in the houses of the rich. Piped water was installed at Richmond Palace, and at Hardwick House a horse-wheel powered pump fed water to a special room beside a new hall.

But Richmond Palace and Hardwick House were a bit unusual. Life in the houses of most noblemen improved more slowly; at least in the great halls the rushes were now changed once a month, instead of new rushes just being layed on top of the old, as in the Middle Ages. There's a description of a hall eighty years later – things are still very basic: marrow bones, scraps of food and dog mess are still trodden into the rushes, there are litters of kittens on the chairs, hawks' hoods, bells and hats full of pheasants eggs on the tables, and the whole place is swarming with hawks, hounds, spaniels and terriers.

Many cottages had a single downstairs room. The furniture of a poor family might be just a few stools, a trestle table, a straw mattress, a fire with an iron cooking pot and a beaten earth floor. There would probably be a few chickens scratching about and possibly the odd cat or dog.

"THINGS I WANT – SOME COMFY NEW THINGS"
BY A TUDOR

IMPORTED PILE CARPETS

CUPS MADE OF PEWTER INSTEAD OF WOOD.

FEATHER BEDS INSTEAD OF STRAW PALLETS.

CHIMNEYS

These were still very rare and definitely a luxury.

LIFE AT THE BOTTOM

In 1597 one of the first flush toilets in the world was installed in Richmond Palace for Elizabeth's personal use. It was designed by her godson, Sir John Harington.

For a long time not many people followed her example, and there was still a lot of 'pissing in chimneys'. The rich might have a cupboard or stool-house next to their bedroom with a chamber pot inside which had to be emptied frequently.

But most people used earth toilets, where a bucket full of earth or cinders was thrown down the hole after use

to cover up the waste . Many earth toilets had more than one hole to make best use of the space beneath. Every few weeks or months a 'nightsoil' man would come and

---

Some toilets never got cleaned out properly; modern specialist historians investigate the dried out waste beneath old toilets, looking for things which may have been dropped in by accident.

dig out the waste and remove it on a cart.

There were no proper sewage pipes to carry away liquid sewage, which might leak anywhere. Drinking water from wells was often polluted, and so much muck flowed into the river Thames that clothes washed in it smelled of sewage afterwards.

Some waste products had their uses however. Toilets often had a small extra hole with a pan underneath to collect the urine. The urine was used to make lye, which was used for washing clothes. It was specially good for getting rid of greasy stains. Other things used to make lye included pigeon or hen dung, bran and wood-ash. Apple-wood ash gave the whitest wash.

Clothes were folded into a wooden tub. The lye was poured over the clothes, squidged around a bit, then drawn off at the bottom through a tap. This process was repeated until the lye came through clean.

LEISURE PLEASURES

HAVING FUN, THE TUDOR WAY!

– BUT FIRST, A TIME TO DINE

Elizabeth hated getting up early. She liked to laze in bed till late in the morning, then she nibbled a breakfast of white bread and butter with a meat soup and either wine or beer. Nothing made her more grumpy than to give her strong beer; she had weak beer specially brewed.

Dinner was the meal that mattered. It started at midday or even earlier. Among the upper classes it could go on for three hours. The laying of the royal dinner table was a major procedure. Special officials spread the cloth, carried the bread and other tasks. They bowed and knelt as if the queen were present,

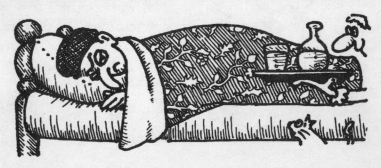

and there was more bowing when she arrived. She removed all her rings and washed her hands in a gold basin before she ate.

The food, when it came, was often cold. Kitchens tended to be in separate buildings because of the danger of fire. At Windsor, meals were sometimes cooked in a public oven in town, more than ten minutes walk away.

Poison! beware!

Dishes were brought to the royal table by servants called the *yeomen of the guard*. As they entered the room, a lady with a tasting-fork made each yeoman eat a piece of the food he was carrying to test it for poison.

Meat with your meat

Elizabethans ate mountains of meat if they could afford it. As well as all the animals people eat today, they ate hedgehogs, heron, peacocks and song birds. In fact they ate pretty well anything with legs or wings except insects. Different types of meat were thought to have different effects on the eater; beef was good for Englishmen because it was thought to be lusty and lively, but hare was meant to make you feel depressed.

Meat was boiled, roasted, baked in pies and made into jelly, which was very popular. Roast meat was turned on a spit before the fire. Often dogs turned the spits by running in dog wheels. Hot coals were sometimes put beneath their paws to make them run faster.

By old church tradition, Fridays and Saturdays were fish days when it was forbidden to eat meat. In 1560,

BAD MANNERS. HOW TO BE RUDE AT THE COURT OF QUEEN ELIZABETH...

WIPE MOUTH WITH SLEEVE

DRINK TOO MUCH

BLOW NOSE ON KNAPKIN

WOODEN TRENCHER

GREAT SALT

Wednesday became a fish day as well. This was so that fishermen could sell more fish. Fishermen were needed by the government because they could be used as sailors in time of war.

GETTING STUFFED

While the rich were stuffing themselves with meat, wine and beer at three hour lunch breaks, ordinary people were – stuffing themselves as well. Foreigners were amazed at the amount of food English people could cram down their throats, especially Londoners who ate more meat than country people.

And country people, although their diet was more limited than Londoners', still ate better than people on the continent of Europe. Some English peasants ate better than German nobility according to one German

visitor, even though poor cottagers and labourers ate very little meat. The poor lived mainly on bread made from rye or barley flour and 'white meats' which was the term for dairy products with the occasional chicken or piece of bacon.

And what did people drink to slosh it all down? Beer! Everyone drank it, for breakfast, dinner and supper. Even children could drink as much beer as they liked if it was available. Normally people drank from horn beakers or black leather 'jacks'. They drank wine too but it was more expensive.

TUDOR TALE:

HOW THE POTATO WAS MISUNDERSTOOD

Most people think it was Elizabeth's favourite Sir Walter Raleigh, who introduced the potato to Britain, but it was in fact his friend, mathematician Thomas Harriot. Thomas had gone to America to help start the colony of Virginia, which was Walter Raleigh's pet project.

One day Elizabeth's chamberlain invited some nobles to try Harriot's new vegetable. However no one knew how to cook it. They used the leaves and stems (which are mildly poisonous) and left the potatoes in the ground. All the guests left with stomach aches. The potato didn't recover its reputation for more than a hundred years.

SWEET TREATS

Elizabeth, like most top Tudors, loved sweets. There was less honey around than there used to be because her father had closed down the monasteries; the monks had needed a lot of bees to make beeswax for monastery candles.

Honey had been the traditional sweetener, so a new source of sweetness was needed. Starting in the 1540s, sugar was produced in London. Coarse imported sugar was purified into large white lumps of up to six kilos each. These were then modelled by skilled cooks into fantastic sugary creations. The cooks could model birds, animals and fruit out of sugar. Even plates, playing cards and wine glasses could be made, using a crisp type of sugar known as sugar plate. They might be decorated with paint, penwork and gilding.

The amount of sugar eaten in England would have been about half a kilo per person per year – if most of it had not been eaten by the likes of Elizabeth, who ate far too much. The result was terrible tooth decay for top people. Elizabeth ended her life with a row of black rotten stumps in her mouth, and so did many others.

RECIPE FOR TOOTHPASTE

Rub ashes of rosemary or powdered alabaster onto your teeth with your finger.

TUDOR TIME-OFF

Elizabethans loved games and holidays, but Puritans, who were extreme Protestants, thought they were all the work of the devil. Elizabeth was no Puritan; she still joined in the festivities on Mayday, even when she was an old lady.

DEVIL'S DIARY

THE WEEK AFTER EASTER

On Hoch Monday, the day after Easter, the men of Reading would grab the women and hold them captive until they paid a ransom. On Hoch Tuesday the women did the same to the men.

MAY 1ST

On Mayday people would bring a tree into their town or village, pulled by oxen. The tree was decorated with flowers and herbs and set upright. There was a wild party which went on all day and night.

NOVEMBER 17TH - JOUST A MINUTE

A public holiday was held each year on the date Elizabeth came to the throne, Accession Day. There was always jousting. Courtiers, mounted on massive horses, rode at each other at full gallop and were given points according to where their lances struck.

DECEMBER 25TH

The festivities at Christmas went on for twelve days. There were no Christmas trees. Instead there was a Yule Log, a massive log big enough to burn for twelve days. The peasants also chose a Lord of Misrule whose job was to make fun of the proper lord and the normal rules of society.

SPORTS FIRSTS

Early versions of many modern sports were played in Elizabethan times:

1. Bowls was the national game and it was played everywhere. Most large houses had a bowling green.

2. Stoolball, probably the ancestor of cricket, was popular in Sussex. (It still is).

3. Skittles was played in pub yards. It is the ancestor of ten-pin bowling.

4. Fives, which is a bit like squash but played with a gloved hand, was very popular.

5. Real tennis came from France. It was originally called *Tenez* which means 'hold on' in French. Real tennis is still played today. It's an indoor game where the ball is bounced off the walls as well as being hit over the net.

Bear-baiting was popular with all classes of people. Elizabeth loved it. She even kept a team of bears to use in her own bear-pit. People would set fierce dogs on us, and we fought them off with our claws. Some of us became famous, like me and my friends Little Bess of Bromley and George Stone.

The Elizabethan Echo

Circulation 2 million

Sports Review

Fierce Football

Football was very popular. Big matches could be terrifying, because there were few rules in early football. In Pembrokshire they played with a hard wooden ball, boiled in fat to make it slippery. There were as many as a thousand players on each side. They cut their hair and beards short so that the opposing team couldn't get a grip on them. People suffered dreadful injuries in football games.

Bishop in Rabbit Ban Row

Golf was already popular in Scotland. The Archbishop of St Andrews had to limit rabbit warren construction on the St Andrew's Golf Links to allow space for golf, football and archery.

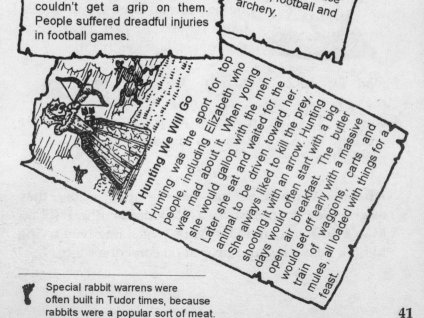

A Hunting We Will Go

Hunting was the sport for top people, including Elizabeth who was mad about it. When young she would gallop with the men. Later she sat and waited for the animal to be driven toward her. She always liked to kill the prey, shooting it with an arrow. Hunting days would often start with a big open air breakfast. The butler would set off early with a massive train of waggons, carts and mules, all loaded with things for a feast.

Special rabbit warrens were often built in Tudor times, because rabbits were a popular sort of meat.

Elizabethans loved music and dancing, whether it was mad dancing behind a Lord of Misrule, or stately dancing at court, normally after supper. Dancing was Elizabeth's main form of exercise.

TOP OF THE TUDOR POPS

Thomas Tallis, 1505-85 was the tutor of *William Byrd*. He held an honorary position, 'gentleman of the royal chapel', which gave him time to compose. He wrote mainly church music, but some other tunes as well.

William Byrd, c.1543-1623. Although he was a Catholic, he became organist of Lincoln Cathedral, which was Protestant Church of England like all English cathedrals. Later he became joint organist of the royal chapel with Tallis.

John Dowland, 1563-1626. He played the lute and wrote songs. He also travelled a lot, working for eight years as a lutenist at the Danish court.

At court, if there was no dancing after supper, they might play games such as Hoodman Blind (Blind Man's Buff) or Dun in the Mire, which involved trying to lift a heavy log and drop it on someone's toes.

DASHING DUDLEY DEMON LOVER

FANCY CLOTHES AND FREE WOMEN

From day one of her reign Elizabeth made sure she was in control of her court. Everyone had to bow or curtsey and to show proper respect.

She was hardly ever alone. Even at night one of her ladies in waiting would sleep in the room with her, and four chamber maids would be on call. There was always the threat of danger; once a mad sailor holding a dagger burst into her chamber. Fortunately it turned out that he was only mad with love for her.

Elizabeth's closest companions were her maids-of-honour. They were a loud bunch of young noblewomen, who used to fool about in their bedroom at night and annoy the Vice-Chamberlain, Sir William Knollys, who slept in the next-door room. Elizabeth had a temper; she would throw things at them, slap their faces and box their ears when she was cross.

The biggest problem for maids-of-honour was getting married. None of the nobility were allowed to marry without asking Elizabeth first, and she was normally very slow to agree. Any maid-of-honour who got married without asking her was in big trouble.

Elizabeth herself never married. She said she was married to England and she became known as the Virgin Queen – which didn't mean that she didn't like men. Far from it; she wanted all her courtiers to be as handsome and dashing as possible, and the handsomest and dashingest of all was Robert Dudley, known as 'the gypsy' because of his dark skin.

Elizabeth was mad about Dudley. In 1560 his wife (yes, he was already married) was found dead at the bottom of the staircase of his house in the country. People said he had had her killed so that he would be free to marry Elizabeth, but there's no evidence to prove him guilty.

Later he married again, to a woman called Lettuce (another mad Tudor name) whom Elizabeth always called 'the she-wolf'. But Elizabeth even forgave him for getting married, and Dudley, or the Earl of Leicester as he became, was her favourite and one of the most powerful men in the country until he died.

Elizabeth worked on her image like a modern film star. It helped to keep her in power. Her clothes were a part of that image. When she died there were more than three thousand dresses in her cupboards. In public she wore incredibly expensive gowns and behaved in a stately, goddess-like way. Everyone at court was expected to dress expensively, though her maids-of-honour had to dress in black or white so as to make her stand out. All this was for the public; in private she liked to dress quite simply.

RUB WELL MY HEAD, FOR IT IS FULL OF DANDRUFF.

RUFF (STARCH CAME IN IN THE 1570s.)

STOMACHER-STIFFENED WITH PASTEBOARD OR CANVASS.

SKIRT HELD OUT OVER A FARTHINGALE

SKIRT

 A farthingale was a frame made of wooden or whale-bone hoops used to extend women's skirts.

FASHION PARADE – MEN

Men wore puffy pants and a cod piece . They nearly always wore a sword and a dagger. Naturally no one was allowed to wear a sword too near the queen. The clothes of both men and women grew flashier and flashier as Elizabeth's reign went on.

The rapier was a type of light sword. It was as well to be prepared, people were always getting killed in sword fights. Some ruffians would carry two swords and two daggers. When men like this had too much to drink, things could get very dangerous. In 1580 a law limited the maximum sword length to three feet (nearly a metre).

The codpiece was a lump of stuffed material which jutted from the front of men's pants.

Make-up Tips

Court was a paradise for pick-ups. It was full of young people when Elizabeth came to the throne. Everyone flirted and dressed in their best clothes. The fashionable look for women was a white skin, thin eyebrows and red lips. Elizabeth had most of these, but other women had to try harder:

- For whiter skin – a powder of ground pigs' jawbones, asses' milk and beeswax. Or why not try a vicious mixture of white lead and vinegar?

- For fairer hair - bleach hair in the sun, but be sure to keep your nice white face in shadow by using a mask held in place by a button between the teeth.

- For red lips – try red cinnabar .

- To remove spots and freckles – birch tree sap or sublimate of mercury .

- To smooth skin damaged by long use of the above make-ups – apply a glaze of egg-whites, then draw on thin blue lines to look like veins.

- To make eyes sparkle – use drops of deadly nightshade.

- To make teeth ultra-white – rub with powdered brick coral, or powdered alabaster.

The proper chemical name for this substance is 'crystalline mercuric sulphide'. In colour it is bright scarlet.

This badly damaged the skin.

MARRIED LIFE

Aristocratic women usually married in their late teens. They had to marry who they were told to, although marriages completely against their will were disapproved of.

Marriage itself was not so important as nowadays. It was the engagement which tied the knot. For the ceremony a bride would wear her best dress, with her hair down as a sign that she was a virgin. White weddings started in Tudor times.

Once married, women had to obey their husbands, but they still had a lot of power in the home, looking after the servants, managing the household finances and acting as doctor to family and servants, which might involve setting broken bones and treating wounds, as well as giving herbal medicines. There were some jobs for women outside the home as well, these included ale-wife, baker and even ironmonger.

Common women had more freedom to choose their partner than noble women, and they married later at around twenty-five, when they were ready to set up home on their own.

English customs were very free and easy compared to most countries' and women profited from this. It was said to be a paradise for married women. There was very little jealousy, everybody kissed everybody else and even a male guest were expected to kiss his hostess on the mouth. Foreigners loved it. Here are some other things which struck them about Englishwomen:

They ride forth alone and are as skilful and firm in the saddle as a man.

At banquets ladies are shown the greatest honour, being placed at the top end of the table and served first.

Even ladies of distinction drink wine in taverns.

They often drive out by coach dressed in fine clothes, and men must put up with such ways.

THE ALMOST KINGS OF ENGLAND

Elizabeth never believed that women were equal to men, but she was still the freest of all the women in her kingdom. Not only did she curse and swear and ride after the hunt like a man, she also never got married. Instead, she used her availablity for marriage as a lure to make other governments do what she wanted.

There were four men who thought they had a chance of marrying her:

1. Lord Thomas Seymour
2. King Philip of Spain
3. Robert Dudley, Earl of Leicester
4. Francis, Duke of Alencon, a French royal

Nobody believed Elizabeth when she first said that she was married to England, but in actual fact she meant it. Which was tough on Dudley and the other would-be kings of England.

Quite a contrast to her cousin, Mary Queen of Scots, who married three times...

OFF WITH HER HEAD!

Scottish Mary And The Multiple Murders

There were two difficult Marys in Elizabeth's life and they were both relations:

Mary no 1
Bloody Queen Mary, Elizabeth's sister, who died in 1558.

Mary no 2
Mary Queen of Scots, Elizabeth's cousin. Mary Queen of Scots was among Elizabeth's nearest relatives and would succeed to the throne if Elizabeth died.

Scotland was always a headache for Elizabeth, and Mary Queen of Scots was a special headache. Mary was a very tall, beautiful woman, who liked speaking French. She had been brought up in France and had married the heir to the French throne when she was sixteen, returning to Scotland after he died. Scotland always seemed like a foreign country to her.

The Scotland that Mary returned to was sometimes

called 'the arse of the world'. The climate was awful, the nobles were rough and dressed like commoners, not many people spoke French – and worst of all it was full of Puritans.

WHO WANTS MY OLD BOYFRIEND?

PROBLEM:

Every Englishman knew that Catholics would love to get rid of Elizabeth and put good Catholic Mary Queen of Scots on the throne of England.

ELIZABETH'S SOLUTION:

Mary should marry Dashing Dudley, a Protestant English nobleman. This was an odd idea; after all, Dudley was Elizabeth's favourite courtier and everyone thought he was her lover as well (which he may have been). Why would Mary marry one of Elizabeth's cast-offs when he wasn't even royal?

Things would all have been a lot simpler if one of the two queens had been a man, then they could have married each other.

PURELY FOR PURITANS

Elizabeth started the Church of England in 1559 to stop English Protestants and Catholics fighting each other. It was mildly Protestant. Puritans were extreme Protestants; they were in the Church of England, but they weren't happy about it, because it wasn't strict enough for them.

Scottish Puritans were much more influential than English ones. Many top Scottish noblemen were Puritans, and the Puritan Scottish organisation, known as the Congregation, was a powerful force in the land. But the Scottish Puritans weren't happy either.

Here are some things Puritans didn't like:

STATUES AND PAINTINGS IN CHURCHES

MAKING THE SIGN OF THE CROSS

BISHOPS

WEDDING RINGS

MINISTERS DRINKING AND GAMBLING

COLOURFUL CLOTHES

DANCING

WELL DARN IT, DARNLEY!

Alright, so Mary wouldn't marry
Dudley, or Dudley wouldn't
marry Mary. Elizabeth, or at
least her ministers, had another
good-looking English nobleman
up her sleeve. The new noble
was a young, handsome,
six-foot-something charmer who
was four years younger than
Mary. He was called Lord
Darnley, he was taller than Mary,
and even though he was a
Catholic he was ideal – so it was a
pity that his personality turned out
to be so much worse than his looks.

Darnley came to visit and Mary fell
madly in love with him. Even
though her Protestant Scottish
lords hated him, and Elizabeth
changed her mind about him
(Elizabeth was always
changing her mind) Mary
married Darnley anyway. The
ceremony took place on 29th July, 1565.

MURDER NO I
DAVID RIZZIO, UGLY BUT NOT UGLY ENOUGH

Darnley was handsome, but Mary soon discovered
that he was also a nasty drunk brute. He was
sometimes so rude that he made her cry. She started to
hate him...

Mary turned for company to her secretary, David Rizzio. Rizzio was small and ugly but he was a good singer and was fun to talk to. There is no reason to believe that Mary and Rizzio were lovers, but devilish Darnley came to believe that they were.

On Saturday 9th March 1566 Mary was holding a small supper party in her private rooms. The guests were a few close friends including Rizzio. Suddenly Darnley appeared through a private door. He was followed shortly after by a friend, wearing a helmet and with his armour showing beneath his gown, and by some other ruffians. Rizzio clung to Mary's dress but his fingers were forced open and he was dragged away to be stabbed to death with over fifty dagger wounds.

Mary never forgave Darnley and she suspected that Darnley had wanted to kill her as well.

MURDER NO 2
DARNLEY AND THE BIG BANG

Darnley went from bad to worse. He was out drinking almost every night. Mary turned for help to a Protestant Scottish nobleman, the Earl of Bothwell. Bothwell and most other Scottish nobles were sick and tired of Darnley.

Then Darnley fell ill. He was put to bed in a house on the outskirts of Edinburgh. At two o'clock in the morning of Sunday 9th February the quiet of the Edinburgh suburbs was shattered by a gigantic explosion in the house where Darnley was staying. His body was thrown right out of the house into the garden, and the house itself was smashed into a pile of rubble.

The explosion had been planned by Bothwell and a group of noblemen to cover up the fact that they had murdered Darnley, by destroying the evidence. The plot failed in so far as Darnley's body was thrown clear and it was obvious that he had been strangled, but at least he was well and truly dead.

Most people thought that Mary was involved in the plan to murder her horrible husband.

MARRIAGE NO 3
BOTHWELL BREAKS IT OFF

Mary made a big mistake in trusting Bothwell. He now took her away by force and made her marry him. She didn't love him – among other things he was too short. But the fact that they got married made people even more sure that she had helped in the murder of Darnley. The other nobles now turned on Bothwell. Soon he had to flee the country and poor Mary fell into the power of his enemies. They locked her up in a castle in the middle of Lochleven. When at last she escaped, in a boat, disguised as a serving woman, she had no friends left in Scotland. She fled to England leaving behind her son, the future King James of England and Scotland, and threw herself on the mercy of her cousin Elizabeth.

ROW ROW ROW THE BOAT, GENTLY DOWN THE STREAM, MERRILY MERRILY . . .

WHATA LOTA PLOTS

So now Mary, the Catholic heir to the throne of England, was in England. Catholics of all kinds saw their chance to get rid of Protestant Elizabeth and to turn the country Catholic. Elizabeth kept Mary under guard in the north of England, but even so, Mary still became the focus for a series of plots against Elizabeth.

THE THROCKMORTON PLOT

Francis Throckmorton planned for an invasion of England by Spain, a Catholic country, to put Mary on the throne. In 1583 he was caught and horribly tortured. He gave away the names of his fellow conspirators before being executed.

ALRIGHT, THROCKMORTON, START TALKING.

THE RIDOLFI PLOT

Roberto Ridolfi was an Italian banker and keen Catholic. He planned a Catholic invasion of England to put Mary on the throne. The plot was discovered by Elizabeth's secret service and the conspirators were caught – except Ridolfi, who was out of the country.

THE BABINGTON PLOT

Babington was a rich young English Catholic who planned to kill Elizabeth and put Mary on the throne. Letters passed back and forth between Mary and the conspirators in water-proof leather packets hidden in beer barrels. Elizabeth's secret service found out about the plot and decoded the letters. Babington went into hiding but was captured by Elizabeth's agents.

SAY GOODBYE, MARY

Elizabeth had had enough. It was clear from the letters in Babington's beer barrel that Mary had planned to have her murdered. Mary was tried by Elizabeth's ministers at Fotheringhay Castle in Northamptonshire and sentenced to death. Elizabeth was always terrible at making decisions, but finally she signed the warrant for Mary's execution.

On the 8th February 1587 Mary walked into the great hall at Fotheringhay. She had grown fat, but she was still elegantly dressed in a black satin dress. It took two blows of the axe to cut off her head. Afterwards the executioner picked up the head by its red-brown hair, but as he did so the head fell to the floor. The hair in his hand was a wig and Mary's real hair on the head which rolled on the floor was grey. Mary's lips continued to move for a quarter of an hour after her head was chopped off.

WORKERS AND SHIRKERS

GIZZA JOB, LIZ!

BUT FIRST – MIND THAT SLIPPER!

Elizabethan England was young and frisky. As much as half of the population was under twenty, and it was not easy to control them. On all important matters, such as the execution of Mary Queen of Scots, Elizabeth made the final decision, but she ruled though her Council of Ministers.

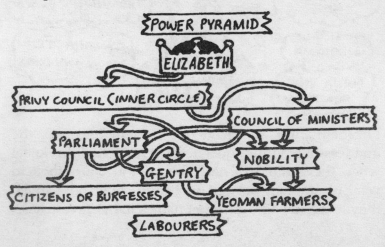

POWER PYRAMID

ELIZABETH

PRIVY COUNCIL (INNER CIRCLE)

COUNCIL OF MINISTERS

PARLIAMENT

NOBILITY

GENTRY

CITIZENS OR BURGESSES

YEOMAN FARMERS

LABOURERS

Elizabeth was not an easy person to work for. Ministers had to be ready to be slapped in the face or have a slipper thrown at them. She was bossy, swore a lot, laughed loudly and marched round the room while she was talking, generally behaving in a very unlady-like way for the time.

Her ministers had to work very hard, but if they asked her for help they were either ignored or made fun of. Worst of all she could never make up her mind on important decisions. Ministers used to rush away with papers after she had signed them, before she could change her mind.

Finally, if one of their policies was successful, they had to make sure that Elizabeth got all the credit – and if things went wrong they had to take the blame. She used to make them really upset: 'God's wounds! This is to serve a base, bastard, pissing kitchen woman!' as one of them said.

NAMES FOR ELIZABETH

GOOD QUEEN BESS

THE VIRGIN QUEEN

GLORIANA

CYNTHIA THE MOON GODDESS

DIANA THE HUNTRESS

Elizabeth built an image for herself. She was the goddess-like virgin queen. Everyone had to kneel when they talked to her. The men at court took to wearing a small portrait of her to show how much they loved her. She gave pet names to her favourites.

CATALOGUE OF COURTIERS...

WILLIAM CECIL, BARON BURGHLEY, 1520-98 HER 'SPIRIT' His mother ran a wine shop. He became the most important man in the country for most of Elizabeth's reign, as principle Secretary of State. She grew very fond of him. When he was weak and dying she fed him with a spoon.

ROBERT CECIL, c1563-1612
Son of William Cecil. He took over his father's job when his father was too old. He had a slight hunchback. His quiet, businesslike manner disguised a love of gambling and jolly dinner parties where his pet parrot would jump up and down on the table.

THE EARL OF LEICESTER (DASHING ROBERT DUDLEY) c1532-88 HER 'EYES'
Leicester was Cecil's main opponent in the Council of Ministers. He was also Elizabeth's closest friend.

SIR FRANCIS WALSINGHAM, c1532-90 'THE MOOR' **(BECAUSE OF HIS DARK COLOURING)**
Elizabeth's private secretary and head of her secret service, a bit of a Puritan.

👣 Moors were Muslims who lived in Spain. They were dark-skinned and came originally from Africa.

Sir Walter Raleigh, 1554-1618

A dashing, handsome explorer and writer who founded the colony of Virginia. He was imprisoned after Elizabeth died,  then was released briefly to look for gold in America, but was beheaded when he returned empty-handed. He became known as the last of the Elizabethans.

Robert Devereux, 2nd Earl of Essex, c1566-1601

More about him later.

Made in England

Elizabeth was careful with money and England in the sixteenth century was getting rich. At the start of Elizabeth's reign, guns were imported from abroad. By the end of it foreigners were buying guns from England.

Floods of Protestant refugees poured into the country from the Continent, but Europe's loss was England's gain. They brought with them skills like silk weaving, linen weaving, glass making, engraving and printing.

Miners were brought over from Germany, so that the English could learn their secrets. Cotton was introduced by merchants trading with Turkey. By 1565 steel was being produced in Kent. A wire-works was set up in the grounds of ruined Tintern Abbey. It employed more than a hundred people.

WHATA LOTA SQUATTERS

Wool was England's biggest export. There were three sheep to each person in the country. The Duke of Norfolk alone owned 16,800. Every year, over 100,000 woollen clothes were sent abroad to Antwerp.

There was a shortage of work in the countryside because so many sheep were reared, and sheep don't need much looking after. This was fine for those who had some land, but not so good for landless labourers.

Families driven from their jobs by the abundance of sheep might put up simple shacks on waste land at night. They had to build their shacks quickly; they had the right to stay if smoke could be seen rising from a hole in the roof by morning. Such families were horribly poor. When John Warde, a Worcester labourer, died in 1608 all he left behind him were his clothes, his working tools, and a few sticks of furniture, with a total value of less than £3.

RAGGED REBELS

An army of around 20,000 ragged vagabonds festered at the bottom of Tudor society. These were people with no legal way of making a living in the place where they were born. Mostly they were labourers who had lost their jobs because of all the sheep, but there were others as well:

O In every town there was a mob of the very poor. They might be vagabonds from the country, soldiers with no war to fight, masterless people or general misfits.

O There were bands of gypsies on the loose, known as gypsies because they were thought to have come from Egypt. They had dark skin and wore piles of rags and rich clothes all mixed up and big gold-embroidered head-coverings. They were thought to be expert thieves and fortune-tellers.

There were laws, dating from Henry VIII's time, to make all these 'sturdy beggars' stay at home, where they were meant to be looked after by the overseer of the poor, and there were specially strict laws for gypsies. But many vagabonds took to a life of crime, to avoid a life of poverty in their home town or village.

STOP THIEF!

It was a hard job keeping control in the towns and villages. The local court was run by a Justice of the

Peace, (JP), normally a local gentleman. He appointed constables from the local yeomen or citizens. It was their job to help the JP and to raise a 'hue and cry' after a robbery or attack. In a hue and cry everyone was meant to chase after the criminal.

There were plenty of crimes apart from robbery to keep the constables busy:

Being a vagabond

Hanging around ale-houses

Parsons who diced and swore

Being sick in church

Drinking during service time

Parent-beating (wife-beating was not a crime)

Incest and bigamy

All-round evil-living

In addition the Welsh were known for carrying off widows.

DEVIL'S DICTIONARY

FRATERS
pretended to be collecting money for charity.

JARKMEN
forged licences to beg and other documents, known as gybes.

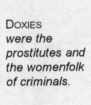

DOXIES
were the prostitutes and the womenfolk of criminals.

CURTSEY MEN
made out they were gentry fallen on hard times.

DELLS
were young girls who were not yet doxies.

PATRICOS OR HEDGE-PRIESTS
performed marriages. They weren't real priests; the couple could separate by shaking hands over any dead animal which they happened to pass in the road.

HEDGE-CREEPERS
were robbers who hid in hedges.

COUNTERFEIT
CRANKS
*pretended
to be ill.*

UPRIGHT MEN
*(they were also be
known as rufflers)
were the leaders of
robber gangs.*

PRIGGERS OF PRANCERS
were horse thieves.

NIPS *cut purses
with a knife and
a 'horn thumb'.*

KINCHIN COES
*were little boys who
were brought up to steal.*

KINCHIN
MORTS
*were little
girls who
were
brought
up to
steal.*

WHIP-JACKS
pretended to be shipwrecked sailors.

PALLIARDS
*begged by showing off scars which
had been made revolting
with arsenic and
ratsbane, or perhaps a
mixture of crowfoot,
spearwort and salt.*

Painful Punishments

Rogues who were caught and sentenced were unlikely to spend long in prison. The Tudors preferred other punishments and also executed about eight hundred people a year.

Thieves might be burned through the ears.

People who held unconventional religious views were burned to death, as heretics.

Vagabonds were branded with red hot irons and could be whipped back to their home parishes.

Thieves might have their hands or some other bit chopped off.

Traitors were 'hung, drawn and quartered'. Before the hanging had completely finished them off the traitor was cut down and had his insides pulled out, ('drawn'). Finally, he was chopped into four pieces, ('quartered').

Thieves were often put in the stocks or the pillory. The pillory was worse than the stocks because in the pillory the hands were held and the victim could not defend his face from anything thrown at him. Sometimes his ears were nailed to the wood so that he couldn't look down. If hard objects were thrown the victim might die.

Women, who'd been thought to have committed a misdemeanor could be forced to walk around in a sheet.

Noblemen were beheaded.

Poisoners might be boiled to death in lead or water.

SPLUPHGUMPF

In London prostitutes might be pulled behind a boat in the Thames.

Women were often ducked in a ducking stool for misdemeanors like adultery. If the people doing the ducking were feeling nasty, this could be a dangerous punishment, and some women drowned.

Women could be forced to wear a scold's bridle if they were thought to nag their husbands or to gossip too much.

LONDON AND LOUTS HARD BARDS

The most important place for Elizabeth to control was London. About 200,000 people lived there, most of them Protestant. It was by far the richest city but it was not a peaceful place. No one went out at night on their own if they could avoid it and if they had to, they took a sword and lantern to defend themselves against the low-life lying in wait. Fights between neighbours often ended with swords being drawn.

Londoners had no time for foreigners, who were scoffed at and teased on the streets. Schoolboys were specially fond of shouting insults or throwing things at them.

Sometimes anti-foreigner feeling blew up into a full scale riot, such as 'Evil Mayday' in 1517 – called evil because thirteen young rioters were hanged, not because of what was done to any foreigners.

The houses were packed in like sardines and so were the people inside them. One medium-sized house in Dowgate housed eleven married couples and fifteen single people!

At five o'clock each morning carts loaded with food would rumble in from nearby towns and villages. In 1581, 2,100 horses were counted travelling on just one road. With so many people packed into such a small space there were bound to be terrible traffic problems, and the number of coaches  and carts made the streets dangerous to walk on. Agressive wandering pigs were another serious danger, sometimes even killing children.

Scavengers and dust carts tried to keep the streets clean, but there weren't enough to keep the dirt at bay.

 Coaches were a new form of transport called after Kotze in Hungary, where they were first made.

The crowded houses were infested with rats and there was a lack of clean water, even after 1572 when a German called Peter Morris designed a pump to take water from the Thames. It was powered by a waterwheel which was turned by the rush of water between one of the arches of London Bridge. At its first demonstration it shot a plume of water right over a church.

> Step up for my terrific tour of Tudor London!

TUDOR TOURISTS

London was more famous than England itself. An English merchant at the Persian court in 1568 reported that no one there had heard of England, but everyone had heard of London. There was a tourist circuit for foreigners.

LONDON BRIDGE was a favourite with its twenty stone arches, lined with shops and houses on both sides. It had the added attraction of the rotting heads of traitors stuck on poles above the drawbridge.

THE TOWER OF LONDON was another favourite, being the place where the traitors lost their heads in the first place. It also had its famous armoury and a small zoo of wild animals.

ST PAUL'S CATHEDRAL towered above Tudor London. It was a popular meeting place where people went to hire servants, show off new clothes or look at the job advertisements pasted on the pillars.

WESTMINSTER ABBEY with its royal tombs was always popular.

THE ROYAL EXCHANGE in Cornhill was opened in 1571 by Elizabeth. It was where merchants went to do deals.

ORDINARY AFTERNOONS

Those with the time and the money would often take their dinner in an 'ordinary' or pub. Ordinaries were very popular. They were used for eating, drinking, talking, card-playing, and dice among other things. Here's some sarcastic advice to a brash young gallant, or man of fashion, on how to show off in an ordinary:

> *Draw out your tobacco box just when the meat comes to the board, rise in the middle of the meal and ask for a 'close stool' (a kind of chamber pot), invite a friend to join you while you sit on the stool in the withdrawing room (toilet).*

TIME FOR ANOTHER?

Since lunch started around twelve o'clock there was plenty of time for a young gallant and his friends to drink beer or wine before finishing the meal at around two. Then it was time for business or entertainment. What could be better than to take a boat across the river to the leisure area on the other side, and maybe go to a play or some other entertainment? The boats often had cushions on their seats and awnings above to protect their passengers from the sun and rain.

The South Bank was the best place to go for bull and bear baiting, and for the new theatres.

The South Bank was outside the city limits, and therefore beyond the reach of the city government. The city government was full of Puritans who thought that plays were the work of the devil. Perhaps they were right – there were also five prisons on the South Bank: the King's Bench, Marshalsea, White Lion, Counter and Clink.

Bear baiting was popular but plays were the height of fashion. As many as 15,000 people per week went to the theatre. Plays started at two o'clock because there was no artificial light for night-time performances.

TOP TUDOR THEATRES

 THE THEATRE, built 1576, knocked down in 1597and materials used to build the Globe.

 THE GLOBE, first built 1599, burned down 1613 and rebuilt 1614 .

 THE FORTUNE, built 1600, burned down 1621 and rebuilt 1623.

Performances were also given in the courtyards of inns and at 'private' theatres, which were used by the upper classes.

 The Globe has recently been rebuilt in almost exactly the same position as the original theatre on the South Bank of the Thames using exactly the same Elizabethan building materials of timber frame and thatched roof.

Elizabethan Theatre

Elizabethans liked their plays to have lots of noise and special effects.

AUDIENCES OF THREE THOUSAND WERE NOT UNCOMMON.

UNPOPULAR PLAYS MIGHT BE HISSED AT HOOTED, AND 'PIPPIN-PELTED' FROM THE STAGE.

MISTS AND FOGS FROM TRAP DOORS

There was often bear-baiting or other animal entertainments before and after plays.

THE ACTOR FACTOR

Actors were known for being heavy-drinking brawlers, boasters, lovers and ruffians. A law of 1572 said that all actors were rogues and vagabonds if they did not belong to an established company run by a lord or high-up person. This meant that they could be branded with a V for vagabond and whipped back to their native town or village.

But professional actors worked hard for their money. One company, the Admiral's Men, put on sixty-two different plays between 1599 and 1600. The Admiral's Men and the Chamberlain's Men, in which Shakespeare was a shareholder, were the two main companies of actors.

Elizabeth and her courtiers loved watching plays as much as everyone else. Shakespeare's company often had to give their first performance of a new work before the royal court.

MORRIS MARATHON

William Kempe, a clown from Shakespeare's company, did a hundred mile solo morris dance from Norwich to London, then wrote a book about it.

TOP TUDOR WRITERS

Some of the greatest
English writers ever
flourished during
Elizabeth's
reign:

EDMUND SPENSER c1552-99,
He was a friend of Sir Philip Sidney. Among other poems, he wrote the *Faerie Queen* which praises Elizabeth.

SIR PHILIP SIDNEY 1554-86
An aristocrat, poet, Protestant and soldier. He died at the battle of Zutphen in the Netherlands, having given his own water to a soldier who was dying beside him.

THOMAS KYD 1558-94
Tom Kyd was the son of a scrivener (someone who copied documents). He was arrested and tortured for treason in 1593. His most famous play was *The Spanish Tragedy*. Died in debt.

CHRISTOPHER MARLOWE 1564-93
The son of a shoemaker, he was the greatest playwright after Shakespeare. He worked for the secret service, was accused of atheism, and died from a stab wound in the eye in Deptford.

WILLIAM SHAKESPEARE 1564-1616

William was the son of a Stratford glover, who married an older woman then made his way to London to become the most famous writer of all time. A rumour started by an unfriendly clergyman said that Shakespeare indulged in heavy drinking with Ben Jonson shortly before his death.

BEN JONSON 1573- 1637

Ben Jonson was apprenticed to a bricklayer, fought as a soldier, became poet-laureat, was sentenced for the murder of one of his fellow actors, but set free by pleading 'benefit of clergy' ◀. He may have worked for the secret service.

FRANCIS BEAUMONT 1584-1616 AND JOHN FLETCHER 1579-1625

This pair were more upper-class than the other playwrights of the period. They shared the writing of their plays. The early ones were performed by Shakespeare's company.

It was a good time to be a writer, but the government kept a strict control on what was published. Before plays were allowed to be staged each had to be passed by the Lord Chamberlain. Nothing critical of the government was allowed.

 If a convict could prove that he could read, he was said to be technically a clergyman and could only be tried by church courts. This strange law dated back to the Middle Ages when only priests could read and write.

LOADS OF LOOT

Posh Pirates On The Seven Seas

Elizabeth's reign wasn't just a golden age for writers. It was a golden age for sailors and explorers as well. When she came to the throne, England was a backward island on the edge of Europe, and English people never travelled much further than France or Italy. With Elizabeth's encouragement Englishmen sailed right round the world, penetrating the icy seas of Russia and the warm seas of Africa, and English travellers roamed across Asia and Turkey.

It's daylight robbery!

There was not much difference between explorers and pirates. If you robbed for the Queen you were a hero!

How to be a robber-hero:

1. Get yourself a ship
2. Rob Spaniards

Privateers were pirates who were licensed to attack enemy shipping (which usually meant the Catholic Spanish), so English privateering was legal - at least as far as Elizabeth was concerned. The Spanish didn't agree of course.

Privateering was gambling for high stakes. It could be profitable, but it was also very, very risky. The financial backers often lost their money, and many sailors lost their lives.

ANYONE FOR RAT?

Tudor sailors were as tough pickled Protestants, which is in fact exactly what they were. They ate and slept in tiny 'messes' of four or five sailors behind canvass screens. They shared the space with another mess of the same number, sleeping and eating while the other mess was working.

Standard daily rations per mess included twenty-five pints of beer. The beer often used to run out or become too disgusting to swallow. Sailors on long voyages spoke of eating candles and rats, of cutting up leather and boiling it for dinner and of holding their noses while they drank stinking water from the pump.

The sailors died like flies from all kinds of diseases like malaria and yellow fever, but the worst plague of all was scurvy, caused by a lack of vitamin C, contained in fresh fruit and vegetables. Scurvy was reckoned to have killed more than a thousand sailors a year at the time.

A VICTIM OF SCURVY

BLEEDING GUMS

ACHING JOINTS

BOW LEGS

The standard large ship for privateers was the galleon. Galleons were quite slim, with a section which jutted out at the front, called the beakhead. In time this became the 'heads' or toilet.

The ships were built by eye. Only the length of the biggest timbers was measured. First the backbone or 'keel' was laid down, this was a huge timber which ran the length of the bottom of the ship, then the ship was built up round it. To curve the planks, they were laid on hot coals and water was sloshed over them while they were bent into shape.

Ballast was laid on planks at the bottom of each ship to keep it upright.

The ballast was normally heavy stones. The galley or cooking space was a brick firebox, usually set in the middle of the ballast area among the rat droppings and smelly stink from the ballast and the bilge water, which collected at the bottom of the ship.

Ships' outer timbers were always under attack from the dreaded teredo worm, which lives in the sea and burrows into wood. Spaniards coated their ships in lime, sulphur and fish oil in an effort to protect them from the worm. The English preferred tar mixed with goat-hair. Neither of these mixtures was much use. Every three months or so ships had to be 'careened'. This meant scraping the hull free of barnacles and other sea creatures and then re-coating it. They sometimes tried to scorch the hull with fire, which could be disastrous.

Sails were huge baggy things made of flax. They were hung from wide wooden 'yardarms', which were often tipped with iron sickles to rip enemy rigging. Galleons weren't very fast, and if a ship wanted to put on speed, the sails were wetted to make them more taut. Maximum speed with a scraped bottom and wet sails was no more than about six mph (10 kph).

The best thing to do in a gale was to run for the nearest port. If that wasn't possible, the captain would order that all the sails be lowered to the deck, or 'struck'. They lowered every thing except the bottom stumps of the masts and possibly one sail at the front or 'bows'. Then they swung the ship round so that it faced into the crashing waves and stayed like that until the storm blew over.

The rudder was moved with ropes or a lever. But the really big problem was knowing where you were in the first place...

HOW TO GET THERE

If they were sailing near to the coast, sailors could steer by local knowledge such as knowing the depth of the sea in different places. In the middle of the ocean things were far more difficult. To help them find their way around, sailors had four main instruments:

Sand glass (turned every half-hour for measuring the time)

Magnetic compass

The 'log', a wooden board attached to a line which was thrown over the side to measure the speed of the ship. The line was allowed to run out in its own time, and the time it took to run out to its full length was measured.

Sea Astrolabe. This was for measuring the height of the sun at noon. Sailors had books which told them how high the sun should be in different latitudes (positions north or south) at different times of year. The astrolabe was hung up on the deck while a sailor stood on the rolling deck and tried to see the sun through a tiny hole.

GREAT ADVENTURE No.1
RICHARD CHANCELLOR AND THE SIX GALLON BOWLS

On 10th May 1553 Sir Hugh Willoughby set sail from London to search for a sea route right around the north of Europe and Asia to China. His  second-in-command was Richard Chancellor of Bristol. Off the coast of Norway the two men were separated in a terrible storm. Willoughby's ship ended up stuck in ice off Lapland, and he and all of his men died of scurvy, cold and perhaps starvation. Their frozen bodies were found several years later.

Chancellor went on alone. He reached Archangel on the shore of the White Sea before winter. From there he travelled overland to Moscow, where he met the barbaric Russian Tsar, or King, Ivan the Terrible, at his splendid court where drinks were brought to the table in six-gallon (nearly twenty-eight litre) silver bowls. This was the start of trade between Russia and England, and on Chancellor's return to England the Muscovy Company was set up.

GREAT ADVENTURE No.2
ANTHONY JENKINSON AND THE HORSE-MEAT MERCHANTS

Anthony Jenkinson was chief agent of the Muscovy Company, based in Moscow. In 1558 he set off from Moscow, hoping to reach the Middle East

overland from the North. He travelled 1,800 miles down the Volga, sailed across the Caspian Sea to Turkestan, then hitched up with a camel-train to Bokhara. Jenkinson described how the Tartar nomads ate horse flesh and loved to get drunk on fermented mare's milk. At one stage he had to fight a running battle with robbers for four days and nights in the middle of a desert with no water to drink.

Jenkinson returned to Moscow from Astrakhan with an armed company of Tartar ambassadors and dined with the Tsar of Russia on the 2nd September, his long journey over at last. He reported that the people of Central Asia were too savage to bother with.

GREAT ADVENTURE NO.3
SIR JOHN HAWKINS AND THE LEAKY LUBECK

In October 1567 Sir John Hawkins set sail from Plymouth with six ships although his flagship, the *Jesus of Lubeck*, leaked like a sieve. Along the west coast of Africa, they helped an African king in a local war and took some prisoners to sell as slaves in South America.

Having sold his slaves, Hawkins was battered by a massive storm in the Caribbean, and the *Jesus of Lubeck* came apart at the seams. He limped to shelter in the port of San Juan de Ulua.

Then unluckily the Spanish fleet arrived. This posed a problem, because the Pope (who claimed to get his power directly from God) had given half the world outside Europe to Catholic Spain and the other half to Catholic Portugal, and the Spaniards did not want Protestants like Hawkins to trade in their patch.

Hawkins let them enter the port, and that night the treacherous Spaniards attacked. Out of around four hundred English sailors, half survived the fight, including Hawkins and his young follower, Francis Drake, but half of these survivors had to be left on the coast of South America due to lack of food and water. There they were captured by the Spanish, and one was later burned to death in Seville market-place.

GREAT ADVENTURE No.4
MARTIN FROBISHER AND THE ANGRY INUIT

The English hoped to find a quick sea passage around the north of America to China. Frobisher was a tough sea-dog from Yorkshire who set out in June 1576, sailing north-west past the massive icebergs and mountains of Greenland. For months he wandered in the freezing, gloomy waters around Baffin Island and beyond, searching for a route through, but without success.

They met Eskimos, or Inuit as they are now sometimes called. Frobisher was very strong. Wanting a captive to take back to England, he lifted an Inuit, canoe and all, into his ship, the *Gabriel*. The Inuit was so angry that he bit his tongue in two, but survived with half a tongue – only to die of a common cold on the way to England.

Frobisher failed to find the North-West Passage on this or two more voyages. But he did bring back a lump of 'fools' gold' or pyrites, which looks like gold, starting a mini gold-rush, in which many people, including Elizabeth, lost money.

GREAT ADVENTURE No.5
FRANCIS DRAKE'S VOYAGE ROUND THE WORLD

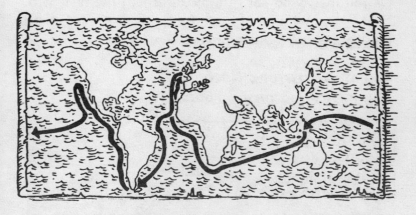

In 1577, Francis Drake, already a top Tudor sea-dog, sailed from Plymouth with a fleet of five ships. Among his financial backers was Elizabeth herself. They sailed across the Atlantic to South America. Fearing a mutiny among his gentlemen sailors, he beheaded the leader, and for the rest of the voyage the gentlemen were treated exactly equally with the common sailors.

In August 1578 they rounded the Straits of Magellan and entered the Pacific, where they started on an orgy of looting among Spanish ships and settlements along the west coast of South America, sailing north as far as modern California.

Then they struck out across the Pacific and sailed back to England via India and Africa, reaching Plymouth in September 1580. They had taken so much loot that Drake's flagship, the *Golden Hind*, was said to be ballasted with treasure. The total value of their haul was about £600,000, a huge fortune in those days, of which Elizabeth got the lion's share.

Of 160 men who set out, 59 returned, the rest died. Drake was not a cruel man; far fewer Spaniards than Englishmen died during his adventures.

GREAT ADVENTURE No.6
RALPH FITCH AND THE OIL POOLS

Ralph Fitch and his friend, John Newbury, sailed from Falmouth to Tripoli in Syria in 1583. From there they travelled by camel and boat down the river Euphrates to Babylon. They were the first Englishmen to see Middle East oil, where it bubbled up in squelchy black pools south of Babylon. Arabs said the pools were the mouth of hell. From Babylon they took a ship to India and made it to the court of the Great Mogul.

At this point Newbury turned for home, but Fitch went on. He sailed down the river Ganges to Bengal, across the across the Bay of Bengal to Burma, then to Siam (modern Thailand) and from there to Malaya, which was the furthest he got.

When he arrived back in England eight years later, he found that he had been presumed dead and his belongings had been given to his relatives.

Great Adventure No.7
Thomas Cavendish and the Plague of Maggots

Thomas Cavendish was an adventurer from Suffolk who in 1586 had copied Drake's voyage round the world. He tried it again in 1591, sailing from Plymouth with five ships – with

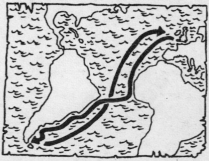

disastrous results. The officers quarrelled, the weather was awful, food was short, and the ships were rotten.

Soon they were starving. Some men were too weak to move and lice as big as beans bred in their skin. In the Straits of Magellan they killed some penguins to eat but the birds rotted, breeding a plague of maggots which ate into the flesh of the sailors and bit like mosquitos. They were forced to turn back.

Finally they got scurvy. Their ankles swelled, and then their chests so that they were unable to breath easily, and finally their genitals swelled up. Some went mad and died in horrible pain. Out of a crew of ninety-one, five were left in a fit shape to sail the ship back to Ireland, eleven were too sick, and the rest were dead.

A COMPANY OF COMPANIES

The Turkey or Levant Company, formed 1581, traded across the Mediterranean with Constantinople. Their ships risked capture and slavery by the Barbary pirates, whose slave-powered galleys lurked in the warm waters.

Trading and privateering were two sides of the same coin. All Elizabethan merchants were happy to do a bit of privateering on the side, as they fanned out across the world in search of trade and plunder. They invented the 'joint stock company' whereby groups of merchants clubbed together to put up the money for expeditions and to share the risk. Here are some of the main companies:

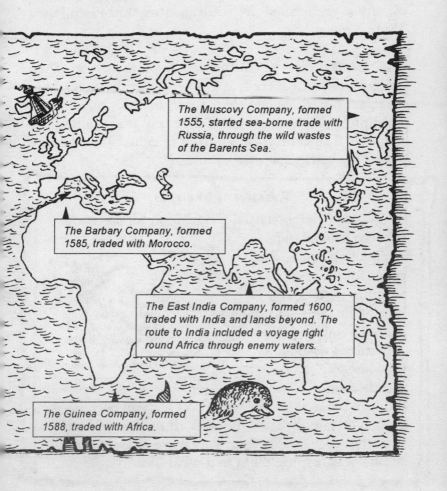

The Muscovy Company, formed 1555, started sea-borne trade with Russia, through the wild wastes of the Barents Sea.

The Barbary Company, formed 1585, traded with Morocco.

The East India Company, formed 1600, traded with India and lands beyond. The route to India included a voyage right round Africa through enemy waters.

The Guinea Company, formed 1588, traded with Africa.

WELL TRIED, WALTER!

Merchants made money by trading with other countries, but it was easier and safer to trade with your own people, like the Spanish did with their colonies in South America.

Handsome dandy Sir Walter Raleigh had a plan to start an English colony. He picked a spot in North America and called it Virginia after Elizabeth, the Virgin Queen.

The first colonists set out in seven ships in 1585. The colony was not a success and a year later they asked to be taken home. Walter tried again in 1587, but it was not until 1607 that a successful colony was planted in Virginia. The capital of Virginia is called Jamestown after Elizabeth's successor, James I.

RALEIGH SMOKE FACT

Sir Walter Raleigh started the fashion for smoking tobacco in England. Elizabeth discussed his plans for Virginia with him while he puffed away, sometimes she had a puff herself. Elizabethans thought tobacco smoke was good for you because it made you cough. They thought all the horrid black stuff that they coughed up was there already, and the smoke was helping them to get rid of it.

ARMADA!

Try Harder Armada

Philip plans an expedition

- O Philip was leader of the most powerful Catholic empire in the world.

- O Elizabeth was Queen of the most powerful Protestant country in the world.

Philip had a problem and that problem was Elizabeth. His Protestant subjects in the Netherlands were in armed rebellion against his army. As long as the rebels got help from Protestants in England they need never surrender. As long as Elizabeth was Queen of England, England would stay a Protestant country.

So England and Spain were in a state of war or something like it for years. English seamen plundered Spanish shipping, and the Spaniards killed them when they caught them – which wasn't very often. It was all very unsatisfactory.

ENGLEESH PEEG

Something would have to be done...

Philip was very religious. He built a palace called the *Escurial* on a mountain near Madrid. It was like a monastery; through a window in his bedroom he looked directly down on the high altar of the chapel.

Tortured by an illness called gout, he worked day and night at his desk in his lonely palace, on papers which came in from all corners of his vast Empire in Europe and America. It was here at his desk that he decided to invade England, or at least force Elizabeth to stop causing trouble.

The plan was simple: gather a vast fleet of ships in Spain, sail up the English Channel, smashing the English fleet if it got in the way, join up with the Spanish forces in the Netherlands, then ship the entire army across the Channel and invade England, where he hoped that English Catholics would rise up to support him.

What could be simpler...?

THE ARMADA

The Spanish fleet which Philip gathered at Lisbon, Portugal, (then governed by Spain) was called the Armada. It was massive:

ARMADA ARMAMENTS

```
Big warships and merchantmen — 24
Other ships — 106
 Sailors and soldiers — 19,000
Cannonballs — 125,790
Guns — 2,431
```

The English fleet was smaller but they had almost the same number of big guns as the Spaniards, and the English ships were easier to steer which meant that they could slip into the best positions for pounding Spanish ships to bits.

The longest range gun of the period was the basilisk, which was up to five metres long and could hurl an eight kilogram ball more than 2.5 kilometres, but it was too big, too heavy and too inaccurate for use at sea. In fact, firing a gun on a heaving ship at sea was like being roaring drunk with a blindfold on; beyond two hundred metres all guns were wildly inaccurate, and if they were fired more than once every five minutes they became red-hot and dangerous to handle.

The English sailors slept below decks on straw mattresses. The Spanish sailors had to sleep outside, whatever the weather, because all the snug places below decks were taken by the soldiers and officers of the invasion force.

Discipline in both navies was strict. Here's a horrible handful of English naval punishments:

Sailors found guilty of murder were roped to the bodies of their victims and thrown overboard.

Men found asleep on watch were given a knife and a jug of beer then tied under the bowsprit  *. They could choose whether to die slowly of exposure or cut themselves free, fall into the sea, and die quickly.*

Thieves were ducked twelve feet below the water then towed ashore behind a boat and left.

Blasphemers *were gagged tightly for an hour until their mouths were all bloody.*

 The bowsprit was the long piece of wood which jutted diagonally from the bow of the ship.

Blasphemers were people who made fun of religion or generally spoke against it.

GALLANT GALLERY

The English fleet was led by some of the most daring and skilful sailors of all time.

CHARLES HOWARD
the Lord High Admiral, a brave,
sport-loving nobleman who
couldn't spell. In fact he wasn't
an experienced sailor – at least
until after the Armada. Howard
divided his fleet into four squadrons. One was under his
own command, the other three were:

MARTIN FROBISHER,
the brilliant and tough
explorer of the seas
north of America.

JOHN HAWKINS
he was the man who
started all the trouble with
Spanish America.

FRANCIS DRAKE
(the Vice- Admiral).
Because of his expeditions
against the Spanish, his
name alone was enough
to strike terror into
Spanish hearts.

Here's some Armada battle scraps I picked up...

Sidonia Stops Corunna Runners – May 1588

Having left Lisbon on 30th May, the dreaded Spanish Armada is reported struck by storms. Spanish Admiral, the Duke of Medina Sidonia, has been forced to put into the port of Corunna, which has been surrounded by soldiers to stop men deserting.

Pirate Spots Spaniards July 29th

Pirate Thomas Fleming was today first to spot the dreaded Spanish Armada off the Scilly Isles. He sped to Plymouth under full sail to warn Vice-Admiral Francis Drake. Drake is reported to have been playing bowls at the time. The English fleet is now leaving harbour, but the wind is against them. Fast one Fleming!

Battle Beacon Warns Britons – Friday July 29th

Following Fleming's news of the Armada, beacons have been lit on high hills across the country, spreading the news and putting bold Britains everywhere on battle alert.

Militia Men on the March – Stop Press!

The Council of War has ordered an army of 20,000 men to gather at Tilbury and bar the road to London, in case Spanish invaders cross from the Netherlands and land in Essex. All over the country our brave boys are getting ready to fight.

The Elizabethan Echo
Circulation 2 million

Channel Battle Hots Up
August 5th 1588

Over the past few days our brave fleet has fought the Armada in a running battle up the English Channel. Being easier to steer, our ships have managed to keep up-wind of the Spaniards, and have sliced up a few slow-coaches.

Spanish Smashed in Calais Carve-Up!
August 8th

In the early hours of this morning English fireships were set adrift among the Spanish fleet cowering off the coast near Calais, where they had failed to meet up with the Spanish army of the Netherlands. Panic stricken Spaniards sliced their ropes and tried to run for it, but the Spanish fleet has been smashed to pieces by our brave boys in the boats.

The Wind's a Winner
August 9th 1588

Due to the strong northward blowing wind up the English Channel, Spanish Admiral Medina Sidonia has decided to slink home by looping north right round Scotland and Ireland with the remains of his fleet.

Losers Limp Home
September 1588

After a truly awful trip round Scotland and Ireland, the remaining ships of the once-great Spanish Armada have limped back to Lisbon. They are said to have suffered storms, shipwreck, starvation, typhus and other diseases.

VICTORY FOR THE VIRGIN QUEEN

While the Armada sailed up the English Channel, Elizabeth sailed down the Thames to Tilbury to meet her army. She went for the white, virgin, look when she rode out to review the troops. She wore a white plumed helmet, a white dress with a steel corset over it, rode a white charger, and held a marshal's silver baton.

News of the great victory reached her while she was still at Tilbury and she returned to London, to streets jam-packed with cheering citizens. At fifty-five she was already an old woman by Tudor standards, but she was at the height of her fame and popularity.

TROUBLESOME TOYBOY

HE CLIMBED TOO HIGH

When she was a young queen, Elizabeth was surrounded by men of the same age as her. It was easy to believe them when they said that they loved her. As she grew old, these old friends died or retired and she found herself surrounded by men who were young enough to be her sons – if she had had any.

ONE OUT

Dashing Dudley, Earl of Leicester, grew fat as he grew older and developed pains in the stomach. He died soon after the defeat of the Armada, aged fifty-five. Elizabeth kept his last letter to her in a jewel box in her bedroom.

ONE IN

Handsome twenty-year-old Robert Devereux, Earl of Essex, was the new star at court who replaced Dudley as Elizabeth's favourite. He had shining red-brown hair, bright black eyes, and he was so tall that he marched round the palace leaning forward 'like the neck of a giraffe'.

Elizabeth was mad about him. They often sat up till morning playing cards and other games. She showered him with important jobs and other favours. But he had to be careful not to look at other women, or Elizabeth might get angry. Once he made eyes at Mary Howard, a maid-of-honour, so Elizabeth stole Mary's dress. That evening she stalked into court wearing it, even though it was much too short for her. "How like you my new-fancied suit?" she asked her horrified maids-of-honour.

People liked Essex. He charged through life like a whirlwind in a hurry. He used to shovel down breakfast as quickly as possible then throw on whatever old clothes his servants handed to him. Unfortunately Essex had a personality problem – he was too big for his boots.

Essex wanted to be a famous soldier. This was his undoing. He had already proved he was a brave in the Netherlands when he was quite young, but he used to sneak off to join military expeditions. Then if Elizabeth ordered him to come home, he would try to ignore her orders. Essex was always sulking and making up. They had terrible rows when she might slap his ears.

Essex had a seat in the Privy Council where the important government ministers met. He was all for smashing the Spaniards at every opportunity. This brought him up against Secretary of State, William Cecil, the most important man in the country, and William's son, Robert. They were much more cautious and careful than Essex.

Who's Top? Essex

In 1596 Elizabeth ordered Essex and Howard, the Lord High Admiral, to share command of an expedition against the Spanish port of Cadiz. 'Lord High Admiral' was senior to any of Essex's job titles, but on the other hand Essex was an earl while Howard was only a baron. Who was more important?

The struggle to be top dog caused a lot of friction. Once, when they had to sign a joint letter to Elizabeth, Essex snatched up his pen and signed so high up on the page that there was no room for Howard to sign above. But cunningly, Howard waited till Essex had left the room then cut out Essex's signature with a knife before posting the letter.

Despite the squabbling, the expedition was a success. Essex lead an attack on the town which even Howard admitted was very brave. They looted lots of treasure and Essex returned to England a hero.

 The treasure included a bishop's library, which Essex gave to his friend Thomas Bodley. Bodley later founded the world-famous Bodleian Library in Oxford.

STRANGE THINGS ABOUT IRELAND

Ireland was ruled by England, but it was hard to control, and being Catholic there was always a danger that the Spanish would try to stir up rebellion there - which of course they did.

The English thought that the Irish were barbarians:

 They lived in huts.

 They were infested with lice. The men used to lie on the women's laps while the women picked out the lice with their fingers.

 On feast days they ate half-cooked meat without bread or salt.

 The poor went around completely naked. Even the nobles thought nothing of it. A Bohemian nobleman travelling on Chief O'Cahan's lands in 1601 met sixteen naked women who, 'his eyes being dazzled', led him into their house. They were educated women and spoke Latin with him. Later Chief O'Cahan joined them and he took off his clothes as well.

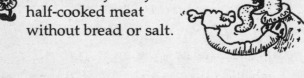

Irish chiefs sometimes hired warriors from Scotland known as 'gallowglasses'. When Chief Shane O'Neil came to London in 1562, his escort of gallowglasses drew crowds. They had hair to their shoulders and they died their vests yellow with urine.

ESSEX TO IRELAND!

The English decided that the Irish were a lost cause. They started to 'plant' colonies of Protestant English families. The settlers thought the Irish were stupid and thought that Ireland was too good a country to have been given by God to such stupid people. The Irish hated the settlers because they were taking the land.

The English governor of Connaught, Sir Richard Bingham, was typical. He thought that the Irish were animals. He took to hanging them, including a one-legged eighty-year-old so it was said. The Irish rose up in a rebellion, led by the Earl of Tyrone, and defeated an English army at Yellow Ford in Armagh. Things were desperate; the English commander suggested using portable racks to torture the Irish into giving away information. Essex pleaded with Elizabeth to be allowed to command a fresh expedition against the rebels. In 1599 she agreed. Essex left for Ireland with an army of 16,000 foot soldiers and 1,300 cavalry.

Tudor armies were full of villains taken from prisons, and other riff-raff. The soldiers' daily rations were bread or biscuit with butter and a gallon of beer. Many foot soldiers had to lug around a musket. These were about a metre long and could fire just one bullet every two minutes. Muskets weighed a ton with all their extras, such as gun-powder and bullets. The English had control of the land around Dublin, known as the *Pale*  . The area under Irish control was called the *Great Irishry*. Essex lead his army outside the Pale but failed to defeat the rebels. Meanwhile his army grew weak through disease.

Elizabeth was angry because Essex had wasted his chance for victory over the rebels. In a desperate attempt to charm her, he left his army in Ireland, sailed back to England against her orders, galloped across the country and burst into her bedroom at Nonsuch Palace spattered with mud, seeing her for the first time with her long grey hair loose. For a moment Elizabeth thought he was going to kill her.

 This where the expression 'beyond the pale' comes from.

Essex was banished from court. For over a year he lurked in his London house, which became a centre for all the troublemakers of London. He refused to apologise properly, which was his only chance. Elizabeth heard news that he was plotting against her, but she had to be careful - he was popular with the Puritans.

So she waited.

THE FINAL ACT

In February 1601 Essex tried to start a rebellion. He set out from Essex house with a few followers, shouting to the people to support him, but no one joined in. The citizens kept their doors firmly shut and the rebels trudged on in silence. Realising that his rebellion was doomed, Essex broke out in a cold sweat. He fled by boat up river to his house, where he was surrounded and captured. From then on his fate was sealed.

Essex was beheaded at the Tower of London on 25th February 1601.

GOODBYE ELIZABETH

THE FINAL CHAPTER – ALMOST

By 1601, Elizabeth was starting to feel her age. She knew that Essex had spoken about her 'crooked carcass' behind her back, even when he was pretending to be in love with her. It was after Essex's death that she took to keeping a sword by her bed, and in her fear of murderers sometimes prowled around her private rooms thrusting the sword into the rich wall-hangings.

But she was still the boss. Her perfumed, ear-ringed courtiers still pretended to be in love with her and everyone knelt when they talked to her, unless she told them to stand.

Her clothes were grander than ever, and they had become a little strange. The French ambassador described seeing her in a black taffeta dress which was open to her belly-button. He didn't know where to look when she pulled the dress further apart with her hands.

Elizabeth was old but she was still active. She liked to ride up to fifteen miles in the mornings, with the mane and tail of her horse dyed the same bright orange as her wig. Then at the end of 1602 she got her final illness.

A DEVILISH DICTIONARY OF DREADFUL DISEASES

It was no joke to get sick in Tudor England. They had most of the illnesses we have today – but almost none of the cures...

AGUE

Malaria or *ague* was common in marshy areas like the fens. Infection is from the bite of certain mosquitoes.

BLACK DEATH

Worst of all was the plague or *black death*, which swept across the country in terrible summer epidemics, snuffing out entire streets and villages full of people. The Elizabethans blamed pigs, dogs and cats for carrying it, but not rats – which were the real culprits. The dog population tended to be killed off in times of plague – which must have pleased the rats.

There were two kinds of plague, *pneumonic* and *bubonic*. Pneumonic attacked the lungs and was the most dangerous, *bubonic* caused black bumps to appear on the skin.

GOUT

The upper classes suffered from *gout*, where the big toe becomes swollen and very painful.

Green-sickness

Young girls got a sort of anaemia called *green-sickness* because it made their skin look greenish. It is caused by a lack of iron in your diet.

Scurvy

The poor sometimes got *scurvy* from lack of fresh fruit and vegetables at the end of winter. This was the same disease that affected sailors on long voyages. Among other symptoms it caused bleeding gums.

Sweating sickness

Flu was a new illness, there was a fatal form known as *sweating sickness*.

Typhus

Typhus, or goal fever, was carried by lice. If caused headaches, a rash and finally death.

Wasting-sickness

Wasting sickness may have been cancer.

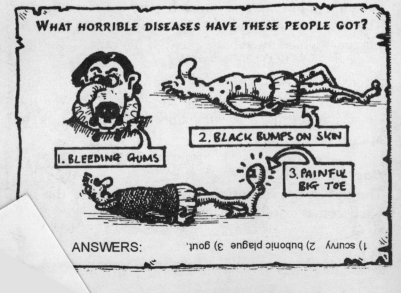

WHAT HORRIBLE DISEASES HAVE THESE PEOPLE GOT?

1. BLEEDING GUMS

2. BLACK BUMPS ON SKIN

3. PAINFUL BIG TOE

ANSWERS: 1) scurvy 2) bubonic plague 3) gout.

Doctors Dolittle, Dabble and Runne

Top doctors were in the College of Physicians. They believed that the body was made up of four humours or fluids - black bile, yellow bile, phlegm and blood. They tried to keep the right balance of these humours in their patients by bleeding, diet and purges. Purges made the patient be sick and go to the toilet. Bleeding involved cutting the patient and draining off some blood. Most of the time the doctors didn't have a clue what they were doing.

Here are some typical Tudor diagnoses and descriptions:

He is infected with melancholy and salt phlegm – breeds worms in his nose of stinking sweet and venomous humour.

She was possessed by a sprite which provoked her to kill or drown herself, and bid her cut her throat..the sprite that was in her said he was a sprite of water.

Troubled to perverse humour of gadding: he would go out of door from his wife and friends without any cause..many times they should not see him for a month or more.

WHAT A BLEEDER!

Poxy Liz

In 1562 Elizabeth had had smallpox, a very dangerous illness which leaves the patient scarred by pock marks. Her doctor, Burcot, suggested an old Arab remedy, which involved wrapping her entire body except her head and one hand in red cloth and laying her on a mattress in front of a fire. It worked.

The last gasp

By 1602 Elizabeth was sixty-nine and a very weak old woman. She became seriously ill with a quinsy, or ulcer, in the throat. It was difficult and painful for her to swallow and soon it developed into a soreness of the lungs.

She sat on some cushions in her chamber for four days, hardly speaking. On the third day she put one of her fingers into her mouth and stayed staring at the floor.

By the fourth day she was so weak and light that the doctors could carry her to her bed without any protests. Her councillors gathered round. They asked her if she would agree to James VI of Scotland, the son of Mary Queen of Scots, succeeding her on the throne. She appeared to agree. She had already written many kindly letters to him, advising him on how to run his kingdom.

Elizabeth I died about three o'clock in the morning of 24th March 1602 . She was buried in Westminster Abbey on April 28th. The streets were crowded with people and there was a general moaning and groaning.

So ended Elizabeth I, the last of the Tudors, the mother of modern England, and perhaps the greatest leader the country has ever had. It was hard to believe that she had gone; she had been Queen of England for forty-four years. Most people couldn't remember a time when she hadn't been queen.

At that time 24th March was the last day of the year.

SO WHAT HAPPENED NEXT?

HI!

WELL, A BIT OF IT

Robert Carey, Elizabeth's cousin, was nearby in Richmond Palace when she died. He walked quietly out of the palace grounds then mounted a horse and galloped up the Great North Road. Within sixty hours he had ridden nearly four hundred miles to Holyrood House in Edinburgh, on a relay of horses which were waiting along the road. He was the first person to bring news of Elizabeth's death to James VI of Scotland, heir to the English throne.

James set off for England within the week, with a large crowd of Scottish followers. The English greeted him happily – but they soon changed their minds. James I of England was the first of some seriously bad Stuart kings; by comparison, Elizabeth's reign was a truly golden age.

STATE THE DATE

GLORIANA AT A GLANCE

KIDS' STUFF

1533	Henry VIII marries Anne Boleyn
	Elizabeth is born
1536	Anne Boleyn is beheaded
	Henry marries Jane Seymour
1537	Edward VI is born
1547	Death of Henry VIII
	Elizabeth's sister, Mary, is crowned.
1549	Thomas Seymour beheaded
1554	Elizabeth sent to the Tower by Mary
1558	Mary dies
	Elizabeth crowned

QUEEN AT LAST

1559	Acts of Supremacy define Church of England
1561	Mary Queen of Scots sails to Scotland
1562	Elizabeth gets smallpox
1562-98	French Wars of Religion
1565	Mary Queen of Scots marries Darnley
1566	David Rizzio murdered
1567	Darnley murdered, Mary Queen of Scots marries Bothwell
	Mary escapes to England

1568	Dutch uprising against Spaniards begins
1572	Saint Bartholemew's Day Massacre
1577-1580	Drake's voyage round the World
1579	Francis, Duke of Alencon, visits England to woo Elizabeth
1587	Drake destroys Spanish fleet in Cadiz Harbour
	Mary Queen of Scots beheaded
1588	Armada defeated
	Dashing Dudley, Earl of Leicester, dies

THE LAST GASP

1597	Early flush toilet installed at Richmond Palace
1598	William Cecil dies
1599	Globe Theatre first built
	Essex goes to Ireland
1600	East India Company founded
1601	Essex beheaded
1602	Elizabeth died
	James VI of Scotland became James I of England

GRAND QUIZ

Now that you've finished my book why not test your Elizabethan expertise? Answers on page 124.

Section 1 – Elizabeth, The Early Years

1) How did Elizabeth's father, Henry VIII, feel about her birth?

a) He was delighted, he'd always wanted a girl.
b) He was very miffed, he'd hoped for a boy.
c) He wasn't bothered either way, just pleased to have a baby.

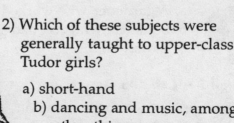

2) Which of these subjects were generally taught to upper-class Tudor girls?

a) short-hand
b) dancing and music, amongst other things
c) horticulture and farming

Section 2 – The Tudor Economy

3) What was England's biggest
   export during Tudor Times?

a) Wool
b) Tabby cats
c) Industrial machinery

4) Who brought the potato to England?

a) Sir Francis Drake
b) Sir Walter Raleigh
c) An angry Inuit

5) What sort of work did Tudor women do?

a) They never did any work outside the
   home.
b) Sometimes they did jobs like baker
   as well as housework.
c) They were at the top of the power pyramid
   and therefore never did any work at all.

6) Who was a nightsoil man?

a) A gardener who worked late at nght
b) Someone who emptied peoples' toilets
c) A dirty soldier

Section 3 – Law and Order

7) Who were known for carrying off
   widows?

a) Welshmen
b) Protestant clegymen
c) The landless poor

8) Who were Upright Men?

a) The leaders of robber bands
b) Protestant clergymen
c) Members of Elizabeth's Privy Council

9) Who was Francis Throckmorton?

a) A Catholic conspirator who was
   horribly tortured after his capture
b) The Royal Valet in charge of
   Elizabeth's frocks
c) A Protestant clergyman

SECTION 4 – TUDOR LIFESTYLES

10) Which of these was a codpiece?

a) A helping of fried fish
b) A men's fashion accessory
c) A type of wig worn by Elizabeth

11) Which of these animals was a top Tudor pet?

a) A peacock
b) A hedgehog
c) A tabby cat

12) Which group of people were especially vunerable
    to green-sickness?

a) People who ate too many vegetables
b) Young girls who didn't get enough
   iron in their diet
c) Noblemen who got their fingers
   stained from counting their
   money too much

SECTION 5 – THE END

13) *Find the odd one out...*which one of these people was *not* beheaded during Elizabeth's lifetime?

a) Queen Anne Boleyn
b) Lord Thomas Seymour
c) Mary, Queen of Scots
d) Robert Devereux, Earl of Essex
e) Sir Francis Drake

14) Who succeeded Elizabeth to the throne?

a) Edward VI
b) The Earl of Essex
c) James VI of Scotland

ANSWERS:

1. b) see page 6
2. b) see pages 12-14
3. a) see page 65
4. b) see page 37
5. b) see page 49
6. b) see page 30
7. a) see page 67
8. a) see page 69
9. a) see page 59
10. b) see page 47
11. c) see pages 32 and 18. (Tudors ate hedgehogs and peacocks!).
12. b) see page 114
13. e) Drake beheaded a mutinous gentleman in his crew but was not beheaded himself, see page 91. The others were all beheaded.
14. c) see page 118

INDEX

Actors 80
Admiral's Men 80
Alencon, Francis, Duke of 51
Anne of Cleves 7
Anne Boleyn 6-10,69
Armada 98-104
Astrology 25

Babington 59
Barbary Company 95
Bear-baiting 41, 77, 78
Beaumont, Francis 82
Beer 32, 36, 84, 110
Bingham, Sir Richard 109
Bodley, Thomas 107
Bothwell, Robert, Earl of 57, 58
Bowls 41, 102
Bull-Baiting 77
Burghley, Baron – see Cecil, William
Byrd, William 42

Catherine of Aragon 7
Catholics 20, 22, 53, 54, 58, 59, 90, 97, 108
Cavendish, Thomas 93
Cecil, Robert 63
Cecil, William (Baron Burghley) 63
Chamberlain's men 80
Chancellor, Richard 88
Clothes 31, 46-47
Crime 66-69, 100

Darnley, Lord (Henry Stewart) 55-58
Dee, Dr John 25
Devereu, Robert, (Earl of Essex) 105-111
Diseases - general 85, 94, 103, 113, 116
Dowland, John 42
Drake, Sir Francis 90, 91, 92, 101
Dudley, Robert – see Leicester, Earl of
Dutch Protestants 23, 97

East India Company 95
Edward VI 7, 19, 20, 22, 23
Elizabeth I
  education 11-14, 16
  image and clothes 5, 46, 48, 104, 110, 113
  leisure 32, 38, 39, 40, 41, 42, 80
  love 19, 44, 45, 51, 53, 105
  old age 5, 110, 112-117
  power and money 7, 25, 43, 61, 62, 91, 92, 95
  religion 21, 22, 23, 39, 54, 58
  teenage years and over 19, 20, 24
  temper 62, 106
Escurial 98
Explorers 88-96

Fitch, Ralph 92

Fletcher, John 82
Food - general 33-38, 84, 110
Football 40
Frobisher, Martin 90, 101

Gallowglasses 109
Golf 40
Guinea Company 95
Guns 99,110

Harrington, Sir John 30
Harriot, Thomas 37
Henry VIII 6, 7, 19, 23
Holidays 39
Howard, Charles 101, 107
Huguenots 23

Ireland 108-110

James I 117, 118
Jenkinson, Anthony 88
Jonson, Ben 82

Kempis, William 80
Kyd, Thomas 81

Leicester, Earl of 44, 45, 51, 63, 105
London Bridge 74
London 72-77
Lye 31

Maids-of-honour 43, 44, 106
Make-up 48
Malaria 85, 113
Marlowe, Christopher 81
Mary Queen of Scots 51-60, 117

Mary Tudor, Bloody Queen 7, 20, 24, 52
Medicine 115
Medina Sidonia, Duke of 102, 103

Navigation 87
North-west Passage 91

Palaces
  Greenwich 6, 26
  Hampton Court 26
  Richmond 26, 28, 118
  Nonsuch 26
  Whitehall 26
  Windsor Castle 33
Palaces, moving 27
Parr, Catherine 7, 19
Pets 18, 28, 29, 34
Philip II, King of Spain 51, 97, 98
Pirates and Privateers 83, 84, 85, 95, 102
Plague 113
Plots 58,59
Pope 90
Potato 37
Privateers – see Pirates
Protestants 21, 22, 23, 25, 39, 54, 72, 97
Pubs 76
Punishments 14, 15, 25, 70, 71, 100
Puritans 39, 54, 77, 111

Raleigh, Sir Walter 37, 64, 96
Religion, Wars of 23
Ridolfi, Roberto 59

Rizzio, David 55, 56
Royal Exchange 75

Sailors 84, 85, 91, 93, 99,
  100
Saint Paul's Cathedral 75
Saint Bartholomew's Day
  Massacre 23
School 12-15
Scotland 52, 53
Scurvy 85, 94, 114
Secret service 59, 63, 81
Servants 16,17
Seymour, Jane 7, 10
Seymour, Lord Thomas
  19, 51
Shakespeare, William 80, 82
Shane O'Neil 109
Sheep 8, 65, 66
Ships 85, 86
Sidney, Sir Philip 81
Spencer, Edmund 81
Sugar 38

Tallis, Thomas 42
Tennis 41
Theatre 77-79
Throckmorton, Francis 59
Tobacco 96
Toilets 30, 76, 85
Tower of London 24, 75
Turkey Company 95
Tyrone, Earl of 109

Vagabonds 8, 65 66, 67, 70,
  80
Virginia 37, 96

Walsingham, Sir Francis 63

Westminster Abbey 25, 26,
  75
Willoughby, Sir Hugh 88
Women 49, 50, 51, 108

Yellow Fever 85

NOW READ ON!

If you want to know more about Elizabeth and her amazing reign, see if your local library or bookshop has these books.

THE ELIZABETHAN UNDERWORLD
BY ARTHUR J. VALENTINE (ROUTLEDGE AND K. PAUL 1965)
All about real Tudor villains by real Tudors. Find out what went on among the Doxies, Dells and Priggers of Prancers.

THE GOLDEN AGE OF THE GALLEON
BY FRANK NIGHT (COLLINS & CO 1976)
All you need to know about Tudor sailors and their ships, including dreadful diseases and disasters, plus exciting adventures.

ELIZABETHAN HOME
BY CLAUDIUS HOLLYBRAND (COBDEN-SANDERSON 1930)
Really mad Tudor tales by actual Tudors on how to behave (and how not to behave) for real Tudor children.

FOOD AND FEASTS IN TUDOR TIMES
BY RICHARD BALKWILL (WAYLAND 1995)
The clothes, the manners, the drink, the dirt – find out how Elizabethans pigged out.

QUEEN ELIZABETH I
BY BETKA ZAMOYSKA (LONGMAN GREAT LIVES SERIES 1981)
Lots of brilliant pictures and fascinating stories. Find out what she really looked like!

A HISTORY OF EVERYDAY THINGS IN ENGLAND (VOL II), 1500-1799, BY MARJORIE AND CHB. QUENNELL (BATSFORD 1968)
The first flush toilet laid bare, and other wonders.